HERE'S TO EWE

Riddles about Sheep

by Diane L. Burns & Dan Scholten
pictures by Susan Slattery Burke

Lerner Publications Company · Minneapolis

To Steve and Kathy Lindahl, and Bob and Kathy Mell—who weave wool and friendships with equal success —D.L.B.

To my little flock, Sue, Rachel, and Nathan —D.S.

To my dear parents, Jean and Jim, for their undying enthusiasm for even the silliest of illustrations —S.S.B.

Copyright © 1990 by Lerner Publications Company

This book is available in two editions:
Library binding by Lerner Publications Company
Soft cover by First Avenue Editions
241 First Avenue North
Minneapolis, Minnesota 55401

Library of Congress Cataloging-in-Publication Data

Burns, Diane L.
  Here's to ewe: riddles about sheep/by Diane L. Burns & Dan Scholten; pictures by Susan Slattery Burke.
       p.   cm.—(You must be joking)
   Summary: A collection of humorous riddles about sheep.
   ISBN 0-8225-2326-4 (lib. bdg.)
   ISBN 0-8225-9583-4 (pbk.)
   1. Riddles, Juvenile. 2. Sheep—Juvenile humor. [1. Riddles.
2. Sheep—Wit and humor.] I. Scholten, Dan. II. Burke, Susan
Slattery, ill. III. Title. IV. Series.
PN6371.5.B86   1990
398.6—dc20   89-36632
                                                              CIP
Manufactured in the United States of America   AC

    2   3   4   5   6   7   8   9   10   99   98   97   96   95   94   93   92   91

Q: What kind of clothes do sheep wear on the job?

A: Ewe-niforms.

Q: How do rich sheep travel?

A: In chauffeured lambousines.

Q: What part of drivers' training gives a ram trouble?

A: The ewe turns.

Q: How does a sheep change a flat tire?

A: With a crowbaa.

Q: What do you call ewes and rams who construct boats?

A: Sheepbuilders.

Q: What kind of trucks do sheep drive?
A: Ewe-Hauls.

Q: What do ewes wear to the beach?
A: Baa-kinis.

Q: What do sheep go
to see at the zoo?
A: The baa...boons.

Q: What do you call the ewes on the sidelines of a football field?
A: The shearleaders.

Q: Why would a little sheep need stitches?
A: If he were bleating.

Q: What sport do sheep like to play?
A: Baa…sketball.

Q: Why are sheep so creative?
A: Because they have shear imagination.

Q: Why don't sheep ever get discouraged?
A: They know that where there's a wool,
there's a way.

Q: Which karate move is practiced by every
sheep?
A: The lamb chop.

Q: What do you call sheep who exercise?
A: Wool sweaters.

Q: What type of munchies do sheep take on camping trips?

A: Fleece-dried food.

Q: Where do sheep go backpacking?

A: In the wool-derness.

Q: What fish do ewes like to eat?

A: Baa...ss!

Q: Who is the strongest sheep in the world?
A: Hydraulic Ram.

Q: What do you get when you cross a sheep with a singing insect?
A: A baa humbug.

Q: What kind of sheep work in the woods?
A: Lamberjacks.

Q: How are trees and sheep different?
A: One has limbs, the other has lambs!

Q: What tree is a sheep's favorite?
A: The weeping wool-ow.

Q: What sheep can jump higher than a tree?
A: Any sheep, because trees can't jump.

Q: Where have the sheep spent the last 365 days?
A: In the past year (pasture)!

Q: What does a sheep put on its hooves in the winter?

A: Muttons.

Q: What does a sheep go sliding on in the winter?

A: A to-baa-gan.

Q: What do grouchy rams say at Christmastime?

A: "Baaa! Humbug!"

Q: What do you call a sheep who gives encouragement and support?

A: A wool comforter.

Q: Are sheep much fun to be with?

A: Yes, they are a shear delight.

Q: Why are sheep always laughing?

A: Because they are always lambing it up!

Q: How do baby lambs drink milk?
A: From a baa-ttle.

Q: What do sheep like to eat for lunch?
A: Baa-loney sandwiches.

Q: What cold drink do young sheep sell on hot days?
A: Lambonade.

Q: Where do British royalty keep their sheep?
A: In Flockingham Palace.

Q: What do you say to a good looking sheep?
A: "Ewe look marvelous."

Q: Do lambs have good manners?
A: Yes, they say "Fleece" and "Thank ewe."

Q: What do lambs like to eat the most?
A: Candy baas.

Q: What kind of candy do ewes like to eat?
A: Baa…n bons.

Q: What do sheep like
to think of as their
favorite ancestor?

A: The ewe-nicorn.

Q: What fairy tale do lambs like to listen to
most?

A: Goldiflocks and the Three Bears.

Q: Where do rams go to school?

A: At ewe-niversities.

Q: What bluegrass instrument do sheep like to play?

A: The baa-njo.

Q: What wind instrument do sheep like to play?

A: The baa-ssoon.

Q: What kind of music do young sheep listen to?

A: Flock-and-roll.

Q: What do you get when you cross a sheep who cuts hair with a coal mining sheep?

A: Baa Baa black sheep.

Q: Do flocks buy anything from mail-order catalogues?

A: No, there's too much sheeping and handling.

Q: How do sheep give away their possessions after they die?

A: In their last wool and testament.

Q: Where do shepherds keep their valuables?
A: Under flock and key.

Q: Who enforces the law in the sheep pasture?
A: The fleece force.

Q: What organization promotes peace among all sheep?
A: The Ewe-nited Nations.

Q: Why did the sheep cross the road?
A: It was the chicken's day off.

Q: What's woolly and keeps falling off walls?
A: Humpty Caterpillar. Sheep can't climb walls!

Q: What do you call a sheep and a horse who live next door to each other?

A: Neigh-baas.

Q: What toy do lambs play with?
A: A flock-in-the-box.

Q: What ewe lost her lambs in the famous nursery rhyme?
A: Little Bo-Sheep.

Q: How do lambs keep their bedrooms?
A: In sheepshape condition.

Q: What side of a sheep has the most wool?
A: The outside.

Q: Where does a sheep put its dirty wool?
A: In a laundry baa…sket.

Q: How does a ewe help her lambs to fall asleep?
A: By singing a lulla-baa.

Q: How do sheep fall asleep?
A: By counting people!

Q: Do good shepherds have nightmares?
A: No, they won't lose any sheep over them.

Q: What kind of movies do lovesick ewes like to watch?

A: Ram-antic ones.

Q: Why are sheep such good dancers?

A: Because they are so fleece of foot.

Q: What does a ram say to flatter his mate?
A: "I hear ewe like me."

Q: What kind of male sheep attracts lots of ewes?
A: A flattering ram.

Q: What do you call an unmarried ram?
A: A baa-tchelor.

Q: What song do rams like to sing?
A: "I Only Have Eyes for Ewe."

Q: Where does a sheep go to get clean?
A: The baa...th tub.

ABOUT THE AUTHORS

Diane L. Burns, her husband, and their two sons spend their summers "on top of the world" as firetower lookouts in Idaho's River of No Return Wilderness. During the rest of the year, Diane and her family manage a maple sugar farm outside Minneapolis, Minnesota. An instructor with the Institute of Children's Literature, Diane spends her time cheering (loudly) at her sons' athletic games and writing stories for children. She also enjoys meeting people and sharing food and laughter with friends.

Dan Scholten, his wife, and their two children raise a flock of sheep on a farm in northern Wisconsin. A graduate of the University of Wisconsin at Platteville with a Master's in agriculture, Dan is a program director for a Christian camp. Dan enjoys woodworking and collecting antique iron, but his favorite hobby is creating puns: "The louder the groans and the more the eyes roll, the more I love it."

ABOUT THE ARTIST

Susan Slattery Burke loves to illustrate fun-loving characters, especially animals. To her, each of them has a personality all its own. Her satisfaction comes when the characters come to life for the reader. Susan lives in Minneapolis, Minnesota, with her husband, her dog, and her cat. She is a graduate of the University of Minnesota. Susan enjoys sculpting, travel, illustrating, entertaining, and being outdoors.

You Must Be Joking

Alphabatty: Riddles from A to Z
Help Wanted: Riddles about Jobs
Here's to Ewe: Riddles about Sheep
Hide and Shriek: Riddles about Ghosts
    and Goblins
Ho Ho Ho! Riddles about Santa
    Claus
I Toad You So: Riddles about
    Frogs and Toads
On with the Show: Show Me Riddles
Out on a Limb: Riddles about Trees
    and Plants
That's for Shore: Riddles from the Beach
Weather or Not: Riddles for Rain and Shine
What's Gnu? Riddles from the Zoo
Wing It! Riddles about Birds